Why Don't Tigers Eat Bananas?

By Katherine Smith

Consultant: Nicola Davies

WATERBIRD BOOKS

Columbus, Ohio

Mc Graw Hill **Children's Publishing**

This edition published in the United States of America in 2004 by
Waterbird Books
an imprint of McGraw-Hill Children's Publishing,
a Division of The McGraw-Hill Companies
8787 Orion Place
Columbus, Ohio 43240-4027

www.MHkids.com

Library of Congress Cataloging-in-Publication Data is on file with the publisher.

First published in Great Britain in 2004 by *ticktock* Media Ltd.,
Unit 2, Orchard Business Centre, North Farm Road, Tunbridge Wells, Kent TN3 3XF.
Text and illustrations © 2004 *ticktock* Entertainment Ltd.
We would like to thank: Meme Ltd. and Elizabeth Wiggans.
Every effort has been made to trace the copyright holders, and we apologize in advance for any unintentional omissions.
We would be pleased to insert the appropriate acknowledgements in any subsequent edition of this publication.

Printed in China

1-57768-947-X

1 2 3 4 5 6 7 8 9 10 TTM 09 08 07 06 05 04

CONTENTS

Any words appearing in the text in bold, **like this**, are explained in the Glossary.

Why don't tigers eat bananas?

Because tigers are carnivores and eat only meat.

Carnivores have special teeth to help them eat meat. The long, daggerlike teeth at the front of a tiger's mouth are called **canine** teeth. Tigers use their canine teeth to grab hold of their **prey**. Their sharp side teeth help to slice up the food.

Tigers each have 30 teeth. Their canines can be up to 3 1/2 inches long!

A tiger's tongue is rough. This helps it to lick the meat off of the bones.

Tigers' teeth can be gentle, too. A mother uses its teeth to carry its cubs around.

Tigers' sharp claws help tigers hold their prey.

Why don't tigers eat their food out of bowls?

Because tigers hunt for their food!

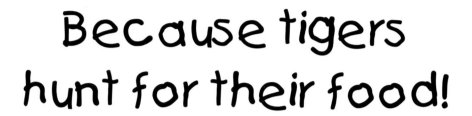

When tigers hunt, they do not chase their prey. They are too big and heavy to run after their next meal. Instead, tigers sneak up on their prey. Then, they POUNCE!

The tiger is the largest member of the cat family.

Tigers can run at speeds of up to 35 miles per hour but only for a few seconds.

Tigers hunt small animals and birds. Occasionally they eat deer, pigs, cattle, and antelope.

A tiger can eat a whole deer at one sitting. Then, it will not eat again for days.

Why don't tigers have spots?

Because stripes help tigers hide when they hunt.

Tigers need to stay hidden when they hunt so that they can surprise their prey. The black stripes on their orange fur help them to blend in to their surroundings when they are sneaking through the jungle. This is called **camouflage**.

A tiger has this special marking called the **wang mark** on its forehead.

Siberian tigers live in cold, snowy climates. They have thick fur, which helps to keep them warm.

Tigers live in the jungles, swamps, forests, and grasslands of Asia.

No two tigers' stripes are exactly the same.

Some very **rare** tigers in India are completely white.

15

Why don't tigers
live in groups?

16

Because there is too much competition for food.

Imagine how difficult it would be to sneak up on someone if you had many of your friends with you! It's the same for tigers when they hunt. That is why you rarely see more than one tiger at a time. Tigers leave scent markings and scratches on trees to mark their territory.

Scent markings let other animals know that the territory is occupied.

Tigers are an **endangered species**. There are only about 8,000 left in the world today.

A **streak** is a group of tigers in captivity.

Why don't tigers
need flashlights
to hunt in
the dark?

Because tigers have excellent night vision!

Tigers use their senses of sight and hearing to hunt at night. Their eyes are specially adapted to see in the dark. In fact, tigers can see six times better than people can in dim light.

Most tigers have yellow eyes, but some rare white tigers have blue eyes.

Tigers hunt mainly at night.

Tigers' eyes glow in the dark because they reflect light.

Tigers use their long whiskers to help them feel their way in the dark.

23

Why don't tiger cubs hatch from eggs?

Because tigers are mammals and, like nearly all mammals, give birth to live young.

Tiger cubs are born blind and weigh no more than a bag of sugar at birth. They feed on their mother's milk for the first few months of their lives. When they are big and strong enough, their mother teaches them to hunt.

If its cubs are in danger, a mother will carry them in its mouth to a safe place.

Cubs open their eyes when they are about two weeks old.

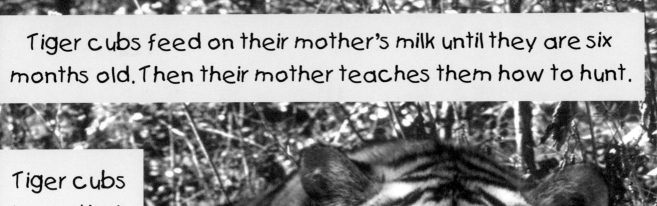

Tiger cubs feed on their mother's milk until they are six months old. Then their mother teaches them how to hunt.

Tiger cubs leave their mother when they are about two to three years old.

There are usually two or three cubs in a litter, but often one dies.

Tiger
PROFILE

Life span

15–25 years in the wild.

Size

6 $\frac{1}{2}$–11 feet in length, which means they can be as long as a big car!

Weight

500 pounds or more, which is three times as much as a male human being!

Numbers

No one knows for sure how many tigers are left in the wild, but it is probably somewhere between 6,000 and 8,000.

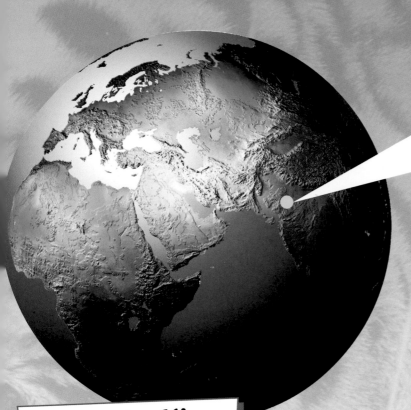

Tigers
live in Asia.

Fact file

There are five different types
of tiger:

Sumatran tigers

Bengal tigers

Siberian tigers (**Amur** tigers)

Indochinese tigers

South China tigers

Scientists believe tigers use
their tails to communicate with
other tigers.

Tigers can weigh as much as three
grown men. The heaviest tiger ever
recorded was a male Siberian tiger,
weighing 1,025 pounds. That is as
much as six male human beings!

Tiger claws are 3 3/4 inches long.
That is half the length of a pencil!

GLOSSARY

Camouflage — Colorings or markings on an animal or insect that allow it to blend in with its natural surroundings.

Canines — Strong pointed teeth.

Carnivores — Plants or animals that feed on the meat of other animals.

Endangered species — A species of animal that is in danger of extinction (dying out) because it is being hunted by human beings, or it is losing its habitat (the place where it lives).

Litter — A group of young animals born to one mother at the same time.

Mammals	Animals that are warm-blooded and produce milk for their young.
Prey	An animal that is hunted for food by another animal.
Rare	An animal that is hard to find because there are so few left in the world.
Scent marking	A special smell left by an animal to show other animals that the territory is occupied.
Streak	The proper name for a group of tigers.
Territory	The area that one animal defends against other animals to keep its food supply and family safe.

31

INDEX